GALOS; Z J

LOVE REVISITED

Passages of Love

100+1 Sonnets

Impressum

Bibliographical information of the German National Library.
The German National Library indexes this publication with the
German National Bibliography. Detailed bibliographical data
may be derived from the Internet website: http.dnb.dnb.de

Publisher:
BoD · Books on Demand GmbH, In de Tarpen 42,
22848 Norderstedt
Printed by:
Libri Plureos GmbH, Friedensallee 273, 22763 Hamburg

ISBN: 978-3-7693-0495-4

pol drwg 01 – les yeux d'un poète

Prolog

As a visitor after twenty years, the poet felt more like someone who had experienced his homecoming.

The poet lived in Athens for three years, bringing out a surge of creativity inspired by the workshops he participated in with local artists.

Before this second phase of a more extended stay in that city, he had visited Athens a few times, meeting with a talented local poetess who had influenced his poetry and art. Since then, the poet has been drawn to her free spirit and her support for growing in his style of expression in word and drawing.

Besides gaining a sense of belonging to his city of choice for art, his studies of architecture gave him the basis for a better understanding of Greek art and architecture. He felt a deeper understanding of it that grew on him with every further visit, especially under the guidance of his teacher and muse.

Twenty years later, he published literature and developed his drawing style for inclusion in his publications, especially dialogues of drawings and poems. This time, visiting the Acropolis, he could hear the temple sing. He had arrived at his spiritual home. Indeed.

The poet felt he had been on a pilgrimage. Had Greek classical art been the cradle of Western civilization, the poet would have felt the same about the development of his art.

Revisiting the places that called for him like a mother for her child, he felt the same for his teacher, muse, love interest, and inner peace of coming home again.

This book was written as a homage to visiting her remains at the First Cemetery of Athens.

LOVE REVISITED
Passages of Life
100+1 Sonnets

I

The body is in turmoil of a sudden oncoming

what is the matter with the poet now?

Have some dark forces turned to violence,

shaking his roots and attacking his health?

Sleep has evaded the poet, who sighs,

pain permeates his body, causing cramps in his

abdomen towards the left side of his kidney

being gutted by a hunting knife.

Sweat covers his body, and sleep will not come

to the frightened guest at the city's haunt of his

adorable muse and possible love interest.

Will he, poet, artist, husband, lover survive

these colic attacks pushing waves of sharp pain

up his urinary tract and bladder?

II

The unusual play of hot and cold weather
has taken its toll on mature men, mature
women and the weather-bent aged folk
the poet hopes to find medical help.

In time, his muse appears, ferries him to the surgery
of Dr R.S, a general practitioner he met through
his friend, the artist of life, and he asked his muse
to accompany him to her practice.

Immediately, he storms into the waiting area
shows his ID to the secretary, who seems at
first somewhat suspicious about an emergency

A man in a black leather jacket with a cap
on his head, long hair stuck up, and a smile
despite the pain in his inflamed bladder.

III

Waiting patiently for an hour, he finally faces
the lean and sinewy doctor of medicine she'll
check his urine and listen to his chest with
her black and silver stethoscope.

Yes, you have bronchitis, she states, there's
also bacteria in your bladder, I'll write you
a script for an antibiotic, please take it for
seven days, and the poet thanks her and

commences immediately to the pharmacy.
He then heads home, and his spouse is
concerned, her hubby has suddenly turned ill.

You have to live a healthy life, she said
eat the right food and don't drink so much
Mr W said that water causes kidney stones.

IV

Nonsense, he replied, and Ina gave him
a lift to reach the surgery of Dr M.D, who
was absent, and her replacement, Dr Las,
had been a temporary replacement,

he checked the poet and found indications
of a kidney stone settled at the edge of his
bladder opening, but he wasn't sure, sent
him for a CT scan in the city of Stockerau.

He accepted a date of 30.04. at 17:30,
but then the nurse had changed it to noon,
and he agreed and headed for the train station.

Come on, poet. Come on, walk to IBD in Stockerau's
commercial area. No, a woman said: take the bus
No.830, but the bus didn't pitch.

V

He phoned for a cab, but no one appeared
suddenly, the bus stopped in front of
the station. Great, you have stopped, he
addressed the Indian driver, who listened

to the poet's story of having such a bad day
with the local transport and the bus not being
on time, and the cab that didn't pitch So,
tell me, why are there no cabs here?

At IBD, he entered reception, where the
young woman was receptive to his story
of an odyssey due to a transport that was

unreliable, but he stood in a queue of four
persons to be interviewed in a glazed in
cubicle of two, so what about being late?

VI

The procedure not explained; he had to
write his Email down to the chick with a
limited knowledge of Internet addresses
he said verbally, handing him a pen.

Now, for a CT scan, he had to sit down in
another waiting area, damned, calls ups
were difficult to understand, but after
taking the wrong cabin, he was served.

The nurse slots him into the tube quickly
he closes his eyes and thinks of his muses
it's a pity she couldn't ferry him here.

pol drwg.02 – the andrologist

VII

At the Klnburg station, he'd arrive on time,
his appointment at four o'clock still stands
well then, he'll sit patiently for another hour
but then twenty later, he's suddenly called.

The Andrologist will check him with an
ultrasound with some problems, but then
the ACT disc shows the kidney stone quite clearly,
size 1,5 cm. Damned! Why now?

"Why didn't I see the stone, or wasn't it here
in January?" Incredible, I thought. Could a 1,5 cm
stone grow in 3-4 months to such a size?

The reasons for this question are to be checked
but the main thing at present is to protect the
kidney, the Andrologist said, still perplexed.

VIII

So then you'll get a stent inserted at first and
then, we'll have to discuss the method of getting
rid of the stone," Dr M-D. said. The poet left
confident that his health could be restored.

"Not a joke," a radiant Dr M-D. said. "To get old
isn't for the meek," he said. She laughed.
"Well, now, you are in good shape for 84!"
that's a great compliment. Indeed.

But the journey for the CT scan still hovered
in his mind and probably as it was one day
after a holiday, everybody was still half asleep.

To travel by train isn't a big problem at all
but to find transportation to the IBD is for
a first-time visitor, a nightmare by bus.

IX

Stockerau, the largest city of the 'Weinviertel'
has no local taxi service and only one bus that
commutes hourly to the industrial area where
the centre for CT scans is located.

Imagine 30 Euro for one ride, for a few km
is excessive, but cabs have to come from the
neighbouring town of Korneuburg. Damned!
Cancelling the cab finally cost him 30 euros.

He wouldn't budge; it was his fault entirely
he'd pay his debt, returning to the train station
the owner of the cab company waited already.

He hadn't been used to the unreliable schedule of the
bus line 830; however, even when he went back to the
train station later, the same thing happened again.

X

At the institute for pictorial documentation
the acting secretary is strict, her voice arduous
but a lack of explanation about the procedure
no distinct pronunciation of what cubicle to enter.

However, once the spot is found around a corner
the calling woman's voice suppressed and garbled
tired from calling patients all morning long, and the
poet dozed off waiting, but somebody woke him.

To be rolled into a tube is somewhat new to him
to the man who was though used to tight spaces
he has no fear of staying enclosed for some time.

It's great to leave the MRT test behind and move
again as a free man with only one problem: getting
to the train station. However, the bus doesn't pitch.

XI

It's no use being impatient in this area of Spillern
that's closer than the train station of Stockerau
however, a sandwich munched for a sudden hunger
will help from Billa nearby across Wienerstrasse.

He had called a taxi from Korneuburg, but the bus arrived
ten minutes later; the driver with pink glasses shaped
like a pair of hearts was somehow familiar to the poet,
but from where? The train station is quite cumbersome.

The train was on time, a welcome change, in twenty
minutes back to the Handelskai station in Vienna,
then take the U-Bahn to Floridsdorf and then?

He could have changed trains before but sat stoned
until his usual station had been announced, travelling
to Spittelau and further by ÖBB-train to Kierling.

XII

The Andrologist attends to him being an acute case

despite this, he has to wait 1 ½ hours for her opinion

about the report of the IBD-centre's DVD, and he'll see the

1,5 cm stone lodged at the bladder's opening.

'How could I not have seen the stone this big

when you were here four months ago?" Well, well,

thanks to Dr Las, who immediately gave him the transfer

papers for an urgent CT scan. Thanks, doc, great job!

.

Returning with the CT-scan DVD, Doc M-D arranged a date

for him to receive a stent and hand him the necessary

Transfer Papers to the Landesklinikum Korneuburg.

There's still time to do the OP; she wanted to take

the pressure off him having to travel forward and

backward. The poet took it in his stride to wait.

XIII

Well, Wednesday, the 1st of May, people march
today on Vienna's main roads, along with banners
singing, and Ina drove the poet early morn' to be
one of the first at KOR-LK urological reception.

But the poet had to wait an hour until a doctor came
despite this, he was determined to get medical help.
The tube shoved up his penis hurt at times in this
mirror search for the kidney stones.

Well, now, at least the stone showed its pebble shape
a black-coloured spot to be seen clearly on the monitor
a first experience with a local anaesthetic for his penis

Accompanied by pains of fire, he'll burn for eternity
had catheters been a strange and nasty experience
he endured this procedure, biting his artificial teeth.

pol drwg.03 – ina & the poet flying

XIV

The operation of inserting a stent into his gallbladder
will be done under total anaesthetics; at least, he'll be
free from any pain during that time, but also a catheter
will be fitted to release the urinal flow.

The poet dreamed of a garden with lush greens
set with an abundance of flowers amid purple and
dark blue, and suddenly, the sky around the
waning moon, artist Anna golden glowed.

She, the artist, drew nature all around her:
flowers, shrubs, high grass, butterflies, and a
bluebird twittered a soft and lovely song.

It was one of his favourites from the
Gershwin's songbook, and Ella sang herself
like a bird, a lullaby of most sweet love.

XV

The poet woke, slept, and woke again
then slept a wink in a room with three other
patients, but that way, suffering was eased
by exchanging their life stories and laughs.

Franz, the businessman, looks like a poet,
with long, curly white hair and a full beard
the Joker is joking, while Dietmar, a pensioner
suffers from a removed kidney, often so restless.

Time spent together with Franz, the entertainer
who creates many laughs and feels amorous
chatting up nurses, hugging cute sister Annie.

A womanizer in a positive sense, a preacher
of the Bible, and a self-made man indeed,
besides being an alert and friendly helper.

XVI

Thoughts will cross my mind fervently
lots of memory snaps will suddenly appear
The voice of Ina: "We married for his citizenship."
The poet's inner voice: I felt obliged to marry.

An obligation?" I hear Ina's voice again. "Yes,"
the poet replied: "We both were intimate for a year
or so, and her mother held me morally responsible
for marrying. Well, love and morals. See?

Perhaps my commitment was split without
leaving a substantial doubt upfront, in my conscious
so then, for happiness, the fields were levelled.

However, the poet fell in love with a colleague,
Bess, an instant turn-on, a femme fatale, followed
him for many years, as she felt his obsession.

XVII

The poet withdrew to end his fixation on her
and it seemed she was pregnant by her hubby
there was more work suddenly for the poet
that drowned all those moments of happiness.

For many years, it seemed to be all but free time,
working, gave the poet a chance for a career
designing factories, buildings, and a competition
entry with ideas for chairs and street furniture.

Work came to a crushing end, but he had a few
years of work left, chancing as a freelance architect
met a poetess on the Internet's chat program.

In times of economic depression, love started
to glow between the poet and his muse to turn
intense to the point of a certain self-destruction.

XVIII

Thanks to the cottage attached to the house
the poet had a refuge in his study and privacy
joining a group of Internet poets in San Francisco
and part of the group thru' a poetess called Blu.

There were times Blu stirred feelings in him
a sensual woman with a history of past lovers
she'd act like a Nordic goddess in gilded armour
beating her drum set, announcing stormy weather.
.

The poet learned to transfer his compositions
to the website of the avant-garde Frisco-Poets
and soon, his poems were read and appreciated.

This World Wide Web-based communication,
the instant magic of a poetry slam brought out
good work and inspired the artist in him.

XIX

creating drawings and paintings for Blu
besides love poetry, they wrote for each other
started the poet's love poems, albeit on wobbly feet
yet it had given the poet love, healing his aching heart.

"Send me your drawing," Blu said, "I like the one
you showed me the other day. "I will," the poet said
while Blu introduced him to her three daughters, who
sent him kisses for bringing joy to their Mom.

Tempus fugit, while he dug himself deeper into his
inside, the poet had immersed into a world that he
solely discovered, and it would be his new love.

While this went on for a year or so, soon he
discovered a chat program filled with a bevy of
young women eager to communicate in love.

XX

One evening in July, out of the blue, a friendly
woman approached him, having read his profile
her name, 'thisevening' seemed to match the time
and his mood for inspired talk and sensual touch.

But then 'thisevening' wished to know the poet
better, before she'd be ready for a kiss and a hug.
This suited the poet, who fell in love with 'thisevening,
who was a poetess, alright, and he told her so.

"You wish to seduce me? Hum, hum." "Yes," he said
"Well, you are in good luck as I have read your
quotation on the web, and here it goes:

Love is the universe, the web, its pulsing vein,
where we'll meet and touch, where our juices flow.
"Thus, we'll meet to fulfil your intimate wishes," she said.

pol drwg.04 – a tête-à-tête below the acropolis

XXI

With such a heartthrob woman, the poet's heart
would join her heartbeat, and he felt and sensed a love
for which he had searched for a long time, and with Blu's
passing due to heart failure, suddenly 'thisevening' appeared.

Her name was Athina, a temperamental woman, an amazon
with a soft heart for the poet, besides being a fine poetess
a runner-up in a national poetry competition published two
volumes of poetry, and wrote a series of short stories.

The poet had won the lottery for his spiritual wellbeing
the poetess would tell him, and one evening, clothed in
strict privacy, the poet endeavoured to denude her.

Successfully, both poets took the first step in love, the first
steps to a holistic love experience that bursts open
the trivial walls to free their innate creativities.

XXII

Head over heels in love for the poet had been incendiary
to Athina's love in words, sound, and telecommunication
as they began mastering cyber-loving, but then the crude
fate of Star-crossed Lovers: a mountain of sweet-bitterness.

On the horizon of a poetess's refuge at a holiday place
of Porto Rafti, where the well-to-do had their hideaways
where lovers met and enjoyed sweet togetherness
at the beach of Erotospilia's paradise on earth, indeed!

The poet had just met his poetess also in person and
enjoyed his first physical encounter in lovemaking at
her retreat, sealing their holistic bond in unification.

Indeed, it had been at the foot of the Acropolis the year
before when Athina asked the poet to enter with her the
ancient Byzantine chapel of Naos Metamorphosis.

XXIII

She stood, a pretty woman in her early forties, a prize-
winning poetess, a great lover, the poet's lottery-win below
the dome's centre, her face lit up by a beam of the sun,
with a gentle glow and relaxed after their first intimacy.

The chapel, now called a church, had a deeper meaning for
her, but certainly to the poet, as if he had just exchanged
marriage vows with her in this unique, sacred atmosphere
just like in a holistic union of mind, body, and soul.

Reminiscing 23 years later on a pilgrimage to Athens
the poet found the closed-up church of Metamorphosis
disappointed, not being able to enter the sacred space.

As if by fate, it had been decided to put an end to
the poet's Infatuation, as it had been a highlight of their
intense love, a consuming fire not to be doused that quickly.

XXIV

The poet's trip to Athens, twenty years after the death of
poetess Athina, he had endeavoured as a pilgrimage to
the remains of a woman he had loved over and above his life
as an architect and an existing marriage that had failed.

Fateful as lovers reversing the sweetness to a bitter taste, the
poet had thanked all his muses who came to his aid after the
death of a Sapphic poetess who endured a metamorphosis
from a free lover, mother, educator, and friend.

The poet had a deep relationship with Greek mythology and
had studied most of it, recalling many tragedies; he had not
felt them more profoundly in his heart before, but now.

Reminiscing at the shiny metal box that held her remains,
he joined the line of her loved ones and people who
were special in her life, grateful to pay his respects to her.

XXV

The poet sat quietly that afternoon after having visited the
spot of her last resting place, musing about life and
enjoying the atmosphere of the quaint, historic environs
of the Agora sitting on a stone wall of the Middle Hall.

Tranquillity flowed thru' his being, transforming him into a
poet of love. Has she fulfilled the wish he had for her?
Perhaps, as the history of a great love played off pic's in his
mind and moved on in his soul and body to higher ground.

Never before had he experienced Athens like this
with a pilgrimage to the places of their love and happiness.
Like Orpheus, he walked the path to her underground spot.

Well, not as hard as it had to be like Orpheus's strenuous task
nevertheless as painful at times of his instant reflections
praying in front of Athina's box A.P.168 at the First Cemetery.

XXVI

A new page had opened for the poet, although he had not
recognized it at first, visiting the Acropolis early morning
in February, as this was their month of the year 2001
when they met for the first time in flesh and blood.

In the Plaka of his heart, where it all began on a foggy
morning, but then it started clearing up and below a mild
late-morning sun, they embraced for petting intimacy
below a cops of exotic trees and an umbrella.

It had started to drizzle. "I have not done this since my days
as a student," Athina said, and I enjoyed her first sweet
little climax, that powerful burn, releasing her sexual tensions.

It would be hard for her, but she awaited her free day when
we could meet for a love-tête-à-tête at her hideaway lodge
for a great event, for it'll be the first real lovemaking. For sure.

XXVII

The poet still recalls all the excitement and sensations
that pervaded him and jumped like a charging spark
over to her body and soul, a first timid try of a jet-lagged
lover eager to please his lover and also himself.

"It is a bit awkward for the first time," she said but enjoyed
to place her legs high up onto his shoulders so he could
easier penetrate her sweet vagina and melt for the first time
in this loving meltdown of two souls and bodies.

The poet loved her; still, it had been an ongoing try
for loving more intensely and more often, limited only
by this age, who could only make it three times in a row?

Still remarkable at his age, the poetess lauded him: " Still
quite virile, my love." She smiled and advanced to ride him
with vigour, tiny sweat pearls showing on her lower back.

XXVIII

He had fallen for her completely, hook, sinker, and line.
Never before had he experienced such sweet love. No other
woman had loved him like this before; even he endeavoured
to love his wife that much on their first night.

There was nothing during his first honeymoon night: from
him a hundred percent, from her utter coolness and a kind of
frigidity he was amazed about, and from a woman who had
sexual experiences, but only the man to be active?

Disappointments in his married life showed the poet
of having chosen an incompatible partner
for his married life, although his Mom used to say so.

Now then, after a life of passing eighty, he couldn't
believe she still stayed with him and wondered about
her Mom's plea: "Please don't ever leave her."

XXIX

Although he fulfilled her Mom's plea, he asked for an open
marriage, where each partner could choose his or her lover.
Through the years, it worked for him but not for her;
she wouldn't take a chance to lie with her doctor,

a good friend of both, but falling in love with the poet's
spouse, then wanting a threesome he rejected. "If you wish to
go, please go with my blessing. She felt for the doctor but
didn't go when he invited her to his home.

The poet wasn't up for becoming a swinger with the
doctor's wife, although that promised financial benefits.
He wished he could be free to choose and become

a man of his destiny and future. That's when Athina,
the poetess, appeared on the monitor of his laptop and
became a star-crossed lover. Though he sensed it.

XXX

"You love me more than I love you," she stated once they
became fully-fledged lovers who lived in constant fear
of being caught together in a lover's embrace and that
put a significant portion of adrenaline into their love act.

"Wow!" he said, "you are the greatest." She asked him to
sit on her bentwood chair so she could ride him in the
total nude, a deliciously sweet feeling caused by her play
of pace, the woman to have children with, but it was too late.

He found himself sitting on a white bench, lined up
along an alley in a significant park, his friend at his side
in a wheelchair with Bordeaux red trousers

a blue padded sleeveless jacket on top of a red pullover
he was well known for mumbling unrelated words of
sexual desires to test the reactions of friends and foes.

XXXI

But the show nobody seems to know more about
Miss Baden on a trained horse with a long-flowing garb
some guys in hussar uniforms on horseback, like the
Kaiser's private guards passed by on an endless loop.

Kicked back a hundred years, nostalgia is still so popular.
Werner checks out the 'Deutschmeisters' from Vienna: "I
don't like the military," Mr T said. The poet agreed. "The split
road of the alley, like in front of our home in Weidling."

Although just a temporary bedsitter, many people like it here
some hide from the law, and some can't afford alternative
accommodation as prices have been climbing for years.

However, all the pomp and circumstance is for the tourists
who flock in numerous groups to Austrian towns with shows
put on for them, especially during the summer months.

XXXII

Panem et circenses, present in history, and that's no news
exactly as Mr T, who says aloud: "Please write down that I dig
women." "Sure," said the poet, "that's fine with me, amidst
the shrieking of a coloured kid who acts as if bitten by a bug.

Indeed, he points to an insect fallen from a chestnut tree
biting the kid, and Mr T asks what all that noise is about.
"It's like a Tokoloshe for him," I said. "What's that? Mr T asked
"It's for African kids what a Golem is for Jewish children.

The bandstand's orchestra plays popular songs and some
Riding Teams show their glamorous wardrobes on horseback
While Mr T and the poet feel hot from the fickle weather.

Or is it Mr T's comment on the pretty Amazons on horseback
showing off the well-trained horses, Viennese Riding School,
at least a well-orchestrated ride in groups meeting their skills.

XXXIII

The cab, called Amadeo, certainly could be a top service
vehicle in Baden, but the driver who was sent to pick us up
certainly isn't a humanist who stood in an upright position
looked at the aged Mr T and wasn't interested in helping.

On the return trip, Mr T got angry and scolded the driver's
unsocial behaviour. "It's not my job," the driver replied with
cross-folded hands showing disrespect. The Spa-Hotel
Baden, recommending them, took it up with the cab owner,´

Add insult to injury, Mr T had a bad swallowing attack, and
some water and a cough mixture rendered him alright again.
I, the poet who helped him, have known Mr T for ten years.

So, with a talk in the Hungarian dialect, he simmers down
from a heated temperamental rise, which, like in the actual
climate, went through a high-low-high cycle. Indeed.

XXXIV

The Spa Hotel is an old establishment that serves its guest
very well, the staff at the café and restaurant is friendly
and the poet has taught a serving lass fresh from school
about the origin of a Hoki fish offered on the menu.

Learning: Daily learning is most important and only good
communication will bring forth a superb generation who l
earned respect, good manners, and greeting with a smile
that immediately sets up a great and super atmosphere.

"I'm here with Mr T for seven days; well, I, the poet, have
taken on a responsibility to look after my friend and take
the load of caring for a ninety-year-old husband

while his spouse rests and recuperates from her tasks
of moving an apartment's contents and storing the
furniture, paintings, books, souvenirs, and all the garb.

XXXV

Besides, the poet's books are moved to 'Waterfield'
in Vienna 2, while Mrs Ina arranged the beds in her cottage
inviting the poet to stay and continue writing his poetry,
and finish his concept of a quadriptych for decoration

of one of the main lounge walls with, given time and peace
to do it. Mrs I will always be close by to care about their
peace of mind, and she'll sleep in her newly arranged bed.
Interestingly, Ina had prepared Mr T's former bed for him.

Fine. The poet is reasonably happy when his muses dance
their elegant and elating round dance, and their laughter
echoes in both of us.

They adore the aged couple who adores them in return, as
both need each other, just like her hired help and
the poet endeavours to relax Mrs Ina's restless mind.

XXXVI

The sun's glow increases in the afternoon while the day flies
and settles in the west exactly, in a dip between two hillocks
abstract brushstrokes create dawn on white clouds that have
brought forward the lover's mirror of an emotional deed.

I'll be happy here in Baden, place of the late Imperial king,
of famous musicians like Strauß, Lanner, Mozart, and
Beethoven, who all resided here in the spa and relaxed in the
'Kurpark' of their Innerness with their fantastic creations.

The heavens were azure blue. A lone airplane danced across
the broad skyscape, leaving a short, condensed tail like a
falling comet, while guests retired after tea, the poet muses.

Gradually, the dense, wooded, dark mountains absorb the
twilight until the black night falls like a boudoir's velvet
curtain, and a chimney stack morphed into a watchtower.

XXXVII

The evening's coolness wraps us in pleasant feelings, the
poet retreats into his part of the apartment, works on a table
next to his bed, where he will render his drawings and write
his stanzas about stealthy love inspired by his muses.

He'll be busy all summer collating his poetry, genuine
drawings for his contemporary books *Art & Love*, seven
volumes of a living journal that shows days in love, and the
doom of Icarus, an artist who fell from his climactic heights.

Night falls in increments of a huge dimmer switch of nature
turned down for the spirits of the night in an eternal battle
of good and evil. The poet on the terrace is writing his soul.

However, as age is creeping up with men and mice alike,
the pretty women of yesteryear have aged considerably
'cept for a lady friend and muse who keeps going very well.

pol drwg.05 - each other's adoration

XXXVIII

However strenuous moving accommodation is, Ina is a strong
woman mentally. She has a first-class mind with figures and
earns five stars in managerial skills. Indeed, the poet admires
a special relationship's silver lining on Waterfield's horizon.

Mr T, accepting age with difficulty, has princely expectations
from his contemporaries, be it cab driver, doctor, or someone
he just met, creating crass misunderstandings and ending in
unpleasant verbal insults on both sides. What a drama!

The poet tries smoothing matters of heated discussions
buying ice cream and curd cake, as Mr T won't accept any
other medication than staging his iron will and nothing else!

This, the poet might absorb and discard thru' his hard-core
shield of self-protection, and supports Mrs Ira whenever
he can, and fully aware of immense poisonous tensions.

XXXIX

The poet told Mr T he'd go to the sauna, his therapy, a half-hour sitting beneficial for his body and soul; he would conduct meditation in this colourfully lit, wood-panelled room with soothing music, open for men and women alike.

The poet had programmed to be at 3:00 pm at the restaurant and take his meal, but Mr T had left his room, moving about with his wheelchair, sitting at his usual table at the restaurant, and having started his lunch already on his own.

"Where have you been?" he greeted the poet in a high voice
"I've been where I have told you, to the natural sauna."
"But we had to meet at 1:00 pm for lunch, Mr T said.

"I wasn't aware of that," the poet replied, "I had to change.
"Just now, we have to see the doctor," Mr T said, moaning about hard carrots in his meal. "It's vital food," the poet said.

XL

The food is only for the health-conscious patients of the spa,
it does not taste that bad for the poet, but Mr T reckons that
the poet does not have both feet on the ground of reality.
Of course not; he is part of another world he has created:

The world of a beautiful garden with trees filled with words as
leaves, waterways playing songs of love, and gentle breezes,
the summer wind whispers words of love; the poet writes into
his red 'Talens' notebook, which he always keeps nearby.

Thank you, my muse of the marble temple high on the rock,
towering over the magical garden for eons of time. Sun-
kissed, he fell asleep. His notebook slipped from his hands.

While he dreamt of his beautiful muse belly-dancing for him,
Aeolus gently rustled the trees; words of love would grow
magic wings, settle like autumn leaves in pages of his book.

XLI

Voila! The dark-clothed woman, dusky-faced, dark thoughts, addressed him while he blinked with one eye at her, perhaps slightly puzzled by his vision of shadows and death. "Is this the end?" he muttered. I still wish to live, write another book

of lyric poetry, you have to sing to me if you wish to address me. "Well, my poet," his muse said, "you should write poems that come to you naturally." The poet said, "Yes, I'll do that, I am, after all, named by you, my muse, *Poet of Love*.

"Yes, my poet, you are. Our connection of body and soul will be eternal from the moment we meet and touch, remember? Love is the universe, the web its p...?" "Yes, I do, "he said.

LOVE IS THE UNIVERSE, THE WEB ITS PULSING VEIN,
THAT'S WHERE WE'LL MEET, WHERE OUR JUICES FLOW.
"See? She said, "Your words have become a reality.!"

XLII

"Flexibility, my friend," his muse whispered and adjusted
herself to fit her body closer to his at the age of eighty-four,
"that's possible if your partner has an adaptable mind set,
complementing both," the poet replied.

Love at a mature age is quite different from the ages of
30, 40, 50, and 60, yet it is quite an experience during
the decades, especially as a poet experiences subtleties
listening to dialogues in love.

The poet is adamant about letting their love grow naturally
in the garden, planted with sympathy and compatibility
he has experienced it ongoing with his present muse.

Love is different from the physical heyday, a pleasant
togetherness that may lead to touches and kisses, and
in times of trust, a vanishing commodity to erotic love.

XLIII

Love in the multiple shades of fine differentiations
will always be a most enjoyable pallet of emotions
comparable to the artist's pallet of colours he uses
for his mystical compositions fired up by fantasy.

ZG, the artist, tuned up in Baden bei Wien to finish
his prepared sketches for rendering and to be ready
for *LOVE & ART II*, which he had planned, conceived
in Athens, Vienna, and Baden near Vienna.

Artistically, it is a well-structured edition of lyric poetry
with 90 drawings conceived at the time of writing when
love was new, and the mind had Pegasus's wings.

Love, once so sweet, fear gripped the heart to lose it.
Love, sending poet and muse on a roller-coaster ride,
intensely adventurous, intuitive that reality didn't matter.

XLIV

Love had drained the poet's life as much as it had enriched it,

firing him up to new flights of ecstasy, playing instruments in

love's orchestral suite, be it Bach, Mozart, Schubert, Ellington,

or Zawinul. Never before experienced the poet tactile love,

mentally, and more soul-bonding than with his muse Anna,

Athina of Acropolis, Ana of Knidos, Αθηνούλα Σάμου –

as her pretty Greek-American first cousin named her.

He called the cousins Athina Power Two; there was a lot

of love between them; the poet had observed and felt it,

listening to them and citing in this loving atmosphere

a love poem or two, well written, reflecting his innermost,

both women enjoyed and related to their destinies

amidst the atmosphere of Fine expressive art and

literature, collected by his Muse Ana of Samos.

pol drwg.06 – making love to the bluebird's warble

XLV

There's a lot of noise near the restaurant, café, and at
various spots where TV sets are placed for public viewing
of the European Championships in soccer, an important
continental event that will connect all the different folk.

Sports and music-panem et circenses – nothing much has
changed since Roman times, oh yeah! Fine. The poet mused
and ate in silence his supper, and Mr T would miss viewing
the competing teams Germany and Hungary.

For the poet, it's peace in a quiet corner of the terrace
where he is shielded from noise within and outside of
the hotel. Gustinus Ambrosi inspired his writing of sonnets.

Recently, he read '100 Love Sonnets' by poet Pablo Neruda
with great interest in love and art, just like he is writing
with the theme of Revisiting Love he had experienced.

(He'll honour the friendship with Mr T, but as his friend
declines physically and mentally, he has taken on a new role of
a helper and supportive partner of muse Ina).

XLVI

Ina, the woman most influential in Mr T's life, happens to fly
in a sideways twist of fortune. The poet joins and befriends
her, and Ina, sporty and active, becomes a great friend who
supports the poet's work without any reservation.

As an artist, he paints and draws Ina's portraits, creates
corners with his painted and written art in her apartment
and weekend cottage she has furnished for herself and the
poet with another bay for an unexpected visitor.

The poet announced his stay for the summer months at
Waterfield 1732 is such a great place for creative ideas
that he became impatient to wait to start his artwork there.

All his concepts emerged a long time ago from the poet's
and artist's innermost, having minimal space available
at the bedsitter-flat he shares for rent with his spouse.

XLVII

At the coming of a road's end, the signal of exhaustion
is thus evident, and the poet's friend seeks a way back
to the days of wine and roses, but they never return, though
happy days are remembered, but in real life he feels pain.

Yet, the poet will, against his conviction, aid the friend's
wishes, his absurd imagination still being strong enough
to turn past times around and live in the past, he'll throw
a party to celebrate his innate madness like a hero.

Crystallizing one's presence, his friend's mind a hard stone
he calls Mr T: Stone, an original species, hard-headed and at
times overflowing with charm meeting young women,

he'll be Don Juan, president, and the Pope's cardinal and
whatever he would do when meeting people in high places
who fell for his hard-core charm, his life's story of survival.

XLVIII

He, Mr T, the artist of survival, a scorned father, not a man
cut out for being a great husband, had ridden a horse of
successful exhibitions, all introducing his venerated father,
who created drawings and exceptional canvases of great art.

His art reflects the Holocaust, the pain, the suffering, the
beating, the torture, and the gassing of men, women, and
children. How could he rid himself of all these horror images?
How could man become a Mensch again?

In this context of Mr T's life experiences, one has to grasp
the fight the poet's friend had to deal with his dooming
family's extinction, yet, days of memento's roses, he'd smile.

While no friends of Mr T are alike, individuals and curious
personalities, critics, and people from all walks of life, artists,
businessmen, poets, and people in places of power.

XLIX

The air is hot, the city for spas filled with tourists and
local well-to-do people, and many elderly folk who
take to the Badener water in the footsteps of Beethoven,
Mozart, Strauß, poets, writers, and the curious folk.

Mr T is adamant to visit the local specialist doctors,
the poet accompanies him, pushing his wheelchair.
His humour keeps him going, and his need to see people,
be it the Café Central or a historic 'Heuriger' in Baden.

The poet has revisited love many times in daydreams,
nights are filled with cries, the faces that meant the world
to him once; however, a glimpse of it will though remain.

Portraits are ever-present: Ana, Ina, Athina, and Irina,
names he still remembers and places their faces on it
but others fell from the clouds and faded into the sand.

L

The poet has lost his heart on the Acropolis of Athens
he sang his ballad in tune with the temple's marbles.
While he closed his eyes for reflection, his muse appeared.
To write poetry the poet has to be in love, Plato stated.

Indeed! Love, at first sight, continued across continents
further upon stealthy meetings that brought forth a bouquet
of red roses and nymphs from the spring of Agora's garden
presented him Athina, mother, friend, teacher, and lover.

The poet's spouse fell from the edge of a steep mountain,
though excellent as a climber, but back then riddled with pain
she had dealt with an incredible series of problems of health.

But then the poet assisted in trying to soothe her emotional
pain and asked her to help him cook a fine meal and serve it
in their apartment's dining room.

LI

In the modern 'Römertherme,' usually, quiet visitors take to
swimming in the half-Olympic-sized pool or crowding the
pool with warm, natural sulphuric water like ducks in a pond
and Baden is famous for, but today, there is no quiet place,

to write down his thoughts and musings, a large crowd of
foreign visitors exercised noisily in the children's pool, a mass
event with loud, stupefying music. The poet will wait for an
hour of digestive time to undertake his routine swim.

Now then, Mr T, in bed with a snore of dreamland, he'd rest
for he'd been annoyed rudely by an assistant manager of the
restaurant telling him he has overstayed his welcome.

The poet replied to the loud-voiced man, throwing his weight
around that his behaviour was out of line. "We are both of
advanced age and hold nobody up from the staff or kitchen."

pol drwg.07 – Love's indian summer

LII

"It's my right to tell you: At two pm, the restaurant closes."
"Indeed, the poet replied, "It's only five minutes past two pm.
Be considerate and tolerant of two elderly people. "Let's go,
Mr T," the poet said," It's useless to fight and become upset.

The poet stated that the manager's tone was unacceptable.
That was all, as Mr T had defaulted, but still, his tone of voice,
staging a verbal fight for 5-10 minutes overdue wasn't worth
it and was an absolute idiocy for a four-star hotel.

It's also tricky assisting Mr T, as he won't accept the poet's
timing, for he thinks to be above the rest, having a fool's
freedom and dismissing rules. "But that's disrespect, Mr T!"

He does not like to hear the truth, and the poet abstains from
firing up his aggression in disagreement with him, but talking
about girls, he quickly forgets about his eruptive-fired anger.

LIII

The poet has revisited love, the drama about his
honeymoon at the Hotel Erzherzog Johann. In love,
just married, the celebratory luncheon behind him,
he looked forward to the night with his bride.

However, the poet is disappointed by BJ's calm
and reserved behaviour that night, which was
essential to the poet, and he couldn't understand
his wife's cold attitude, making love to her repeatedly.

However hard the poet tried to satisfy his woman,
she had placed herself mentally and physically in
a cocoon, and the poet left this debacle half-heartedly.

There's no use in forcing happiness but to take
a person's frustration with sex to that ice-cold state
of behaviour is quite a strange event, indeed.

LIV

During his life in Afrique du Sud, the poet's wife's
unhappiness grew and resulted in her sickness with
numerous operations. His friend and an admirer
of BJ confirmed all the poet's fears for her safety.

His wife had not been tuned to lead a life in marriage.
But then her Mom pleaded with her son-in-law never
to leave her, even if she flirted with a millionaire.
The poet endeavoured to be successful in his work.

Working up his way as an architect, he advanced his
profession to a small partnership, but for BJ, there was
an emotional fix on her surgeon. Fine, the poet said.

"You may leave and stay with him. Please go." But BJ
wouldn't go, why? It had created a risk she didn't take,
but the poet had taken risks and had succeeded.

LV

To no avail, BJ's Mom arrived in Afrique du Sud. She liked
the poet and had him promise never to leave her daughter,
come what may. The poet stuck to his promise, albeit he
foresaw BJ's infatuation with her doctor.

When the poet could sell his professional expertise and
his marriage held up by the skin of his teeth, but when an
economic downturn came around, BJ had a breakdown, too.
Her doctor-in-love had fed her too many tranquilizers.

Not suitable for her health, she grew gallstones, had
to be operated on, followed by another for Reynaud's
disease that would change her life, but she did not yet

realize the dramatic side effects, and yet she begged
her doctor to undertake the operation as soon as possible
having waited for a chance of a lifetime like this.

LVI

Tranquilizers calmed BJ down but played havoc with
her general health and she became ill; her gall became
involved with a few colic attacks. At a surgeon's visit,
gallstones were confirmed to be operated on urgently.

BJ had a problematic time, as she had one week before
her operation when her stomach would be pumped out
of the poison through a plastic tube, she had to swallow
and whereby learn the discipline of correct breathing.

ZJ, the poet, friend, lover, and spouse, had been at her
side at times when he could get off from his office duties,
and he gave her all the support possible, even a 'quickie.'

That helped her cope with pain. At that time, they were
still in love, and the poet hoped that he would make a
career in architecture to earn the fees he had to pay.

LVII

The OP went well, but BJ was disfigured with a vast scar she called 'Säbelrassler' (Swashbuckler). With her modelling career over, she concentrated on caring for ZJ, her spouse, who had to wear a freshly ironed shirt daily to his office.

He represented a firm of architects, and as a director, he had to look smart when meeting and serving clients. However, as he completed his projects satisfactorily, he brought in a new client with a pharmaceutical company and was promoted.

As a shareholder of NNP-Architects, he successfully completed his project for M-Pharma and delivered his speech at the opening ceremony of the factory and offices.

LVIII

His speech was well-noticed, and his client, Jochen, was a *Snappy-nail photographer*. ZJ's former employer, DG, had named him. During this time at NNP, he made a career despite a face-down with 'headless chicken'-Lain, the MD.

But ZJ's drinking problem led to a severe car accident; Keith and his friend slipped a Mickey into his drink, two evil minds trying to neutralize him while under the influence, and it could have been his last party with such ugly colleagues.

His accident driving could have cost him his life, but luckily his car's engine stopped at a steel traverse used as a method of defence to protect the garden wall of a vast property.

ZJ, the poet having sobered up, swore revenge and appeared at a function the next day, much to K.R's dismay—no more drinks, working tirelessly on numerous entrusted projects.

pol drwg.08 – legacy of gods

LIX

This story has a moral: never drink with people who are
the shadow enemy. KR was a sneaky dark horse,
a potential killer who had learned these party tricks
during his time of an illegal stay in the USA.

The poet had been lucky, blessed by the protection
of his good angels, and he continued with the support
of his estranged spouse, who endured a nightmare
caused by her side effects undergoing a 'Swiss-Drip.'

At one stage, the poet intended to leave
never to return as his marriage was on the rocks
and their communication had stopped.

The day his spouse said she'd join her doctor friend,
the poet said: "If you go, never return. Why don't
you go? Do you love him not enough?"

LX

Forty-five years later, the world has changed
perhaps due to the advances in technology
but love has changed as well, and the poet ZJ
and his spouse, BJ, preferred to be on their own.

Fortunately for ZJ, who dedicated his life to art,
poetry, painting, drawing, and looking after his
aged friend who needed a personal assistant,
and ZJ became for Mr T, the person he liked.

However, travelling to Poszony, as Mr T preferred
to name his place of birth, he took the poet along
and they had a good time visiting his friends,

and people from the sciences and the temple,
a portrait painter sketched Mr T, though not that
successfully, and Rita, the maid, blew him a kiss.

LXI

After 40 years in Africa, it's difficult to start over, even
in the country of birth, but the poet wouldn't return to
his country town of birth, having sold his house to a
family from Kosovo, as all his own family had died.

Besides, he wouldn't stay in this country town where
his grandfather from his father's side had been killed by
a blow to his head from two Nazi fanatics. Damned!
The murderers are living amongst us, Wiesenthal said.

Living on their savings, BJ and ZJ stayed in a pension
In Vienna, Kaiserstraße, looking for accommodation;
after two months, the poet had sorted out their life.

Moving to Klnbg-Weidling into an affordable bedsitter
they started to live while working off their past, queuing up in
a social office to secure a monthly support by the county.

LXII

And behind the house at the steep slope's foot
our limbs still hang there where her Mom dug deeper
still humming her songs of love, songs of happiness
and sorrow, and heavenly tunes from her piano play:

The wind carried the sounds away and away
the child, the child, breaker of all her worries,
worried about her youngest child, the man who
often smiled, observing the golden fruit's glow.

Tasting wild blueberries from the mountains,
walnut pies, Dobos cake, fine tea bakeries made
patiently at year's end by sweet Gran 'Lady Basket.'

A starred chef in her own right, she attracted family
gatherings during the main holidays in that town,
considered to be in the heart of Austria.

LXIII

She took me to a place where I could hear
my thoughts feel the red sweetness of her rose
dive into the womb of the Danube's languid arm
nature's closeness embracing body and soul.

Every time I land, an airplane with big hopes on
the twin lawns of her cottage: *il paradiso*, another
person in me knocks at the door; it's my love who
sprung to Bazookas playing Pink Floyd's *Pulse*,

from the seventh column of The Great Temple.
She asked him first: "What kind of a poet you wish
to be known as?" "A poet of love," he replied,

For the flight of time, his capsule of creation has
saved him from the decay of memory for many
years, and Ina, his friend, took good care of him.

pol drwg.09 – ana, anetha, athina

LXIV

The story of his love, the one that changed his life
irreversibly, the poet referred to as his great love,
had a long tale of incredible circumstances he
never has believed would happen to him.

Many years have passed since, he thought, 23 years
since he had met the woman who called herself
'thisevening' on a chat program on the Internet.
How come he had immediately clicked with her?

Becoming friends is quickly done in the electronic age,
but for a friendship to develop means that both
sweethearts have to feel the irresistible power of love.

The poet has called this moment his calling. Indeed,
this moment of being the first time intimate together
sealed the future for his bond with Athina.

LXV

He called her Ana and, at times, Anetha, their love in bloom
and the poet felt no way back any longer and forward meant
the love, unfortunately being a tragic one as written in the
stars, but that fate wasn't yet clearly in front of their eyes.

Messages were flying back and forth from Athens to Joburg
and back with Pink Floyd's music as background, as fantasy
turned hackneyed in making long-distance love, and Ana
suggested installing a camera for visual enhancement.

It ensured a great time with the lovers. Work as
architect receded in Afrique du Sud, but love turned
the married shackles to sweetness and work halted.

Literature and art interests held their relationship
together like glue, despite the poet's obligation
to look after his unhappy and ailing spouse.

LXVI

Spring in Africa came like a storm, just like the
unusual love the poet experienced with Ana, Anetha,
flowering trees in lilac, white, and pink, the list of
happenings in the rebirth of nature, like his love.

Love, at a long distance, is often cumbersome; the
wish for the tactile presence of the loved one is an
ever persistent want to make it become that reality
spurned on the poet to visit Greece with his wife,

who is, despite her nervous condition, a good sport
accompanying her husband, an architect turned poet
and a patient friend turned to an artist of exception.

With many friends around the globe, but only one
he'd burn to meet Ana, Anetha, Athina, the woman
he introduced in Athens to his spouse.

LXVII

Likewise, Ana invited them to dinner, and they met
her husband and their daughter, two pleasant people
who welcomed them in their apartment filled with
paintings and books, poetry, and Ana's literature.

Nobody would have the notion that Ana and the poet
were lovers for years, first at a long distance and now
in flesh and blood. Their feet met below the dinner table,
and seemingly incidental touches aroused them.

Arousal, call of passion, a mapped-out road to disaster.
Ana could inflame the poet, ZJ, in such a way as to hear
a volcano's grumble before it bursts into red-hot lava.

The poet had experienced love's heat and passion
whenever they met, touched, and finally united in
first embraces, which were at the start embarrassing.

LXVIII

Indeed, a red hot needle, her touches bring the
poet to heat and ready to burst into a sea of passion;
no horse, no Titan could ever hold him back to stay
away from Ana, completely bewitched in love.

Such passion, not even experienced before,
perhaps as she didn't respond with the same
fervour, he approached physical love, but then
Ana was the one who blew the top off his being.

The incredible blue and purple: sea, heaven, and mountain,
tarred roads of blistering lava; burst feelings as lava
flowing in the veins of a new, unique, and unified person.

The flight of the century 21st, wings made by Daedalus
better take care and learn from his son Icarus, but in
love the heart overjoyed, flies unerringly to the stars.

LXIX

Where did you meet Ana, Anetha, Athina again?
The poet who lives high with her for 20 days and
one has enjoyed the hospitality of the gods and
goddesses, Athina writes a poem: *A Tear for Zed*.

Indeed! Her tears flow freely, embraced in their
denuded state in a love sit-in on her armless bentwood
chair at her laptop, where she keeps her records for him
to see, observe, enjoy, and perhaps mould his poetry on.

I write these sonnets for my loves revisited
but especially for one that's deeply engraved
in the marble of my soul's stele

of extraordinary beauty, an extension of Rodin's
kiss. Indeed! After all, Ana, Anetha, Athina, the three
beautiful fates, as the artist ZG has created, are alive.

LXX

Alive in the city of Athens, Greece, from the Parthenon
temple at the Acropolis emerged, the most extraordinary
happening, like the sculptures in the National
Archaeological Museum of Athens,

where Z, the poet, the artist of love, had visited with her
at the time of her last two years on this planet, the days
of joy, wine and roses, poems and art, the overture
to the contemporary opera of the *Star-crossed Lovers.*

The streets are glowing coals testing the courage of
Lovers, jay-running the main roads near the library to
the small park, where they jump into the pool

of cold water and ice, fend off the powers of instant
combustion in the August heat of a lover's meeting
literature blooms, poetry thrives, and art is on a roll.

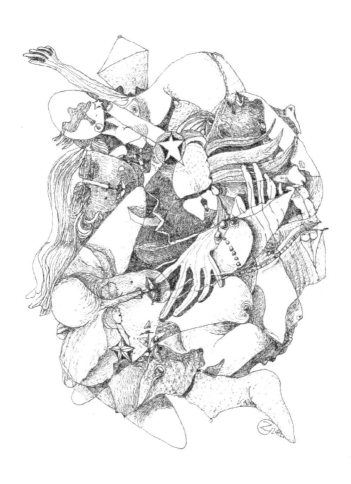

pol drwg 10 – an artist's symposium

LXXI

Who would have thought Z, the poet at heart, the artist
of love, would have to continue on an odyssey? To close
his woman into his arms with a flying Hermes, a silver bird
of hope, rocket vehicle, and love's speedy messenger.

The body of the plane took off like a Harrier jet, fell into the
poet's hair, unkempt and electrified, limbs suspended in the
purple light of Philipappos Hill and its surrounds, this eerie
phenomenon poet George Seferis has described before.

A phenomenon unique to the city of Athens, this poet
Had experienced being in love and reminiscing about a
love with its tenacious, unerring focal point on Love & Art.

Heydays long gone, the poet had aged, Grandpa curled
his fingers in white marble and touched his heart like a
warm human touch, Aphrodite Knidos, just like Ana's body.

LXXII

Forty years after he had landed in Joburg, the dream of making whoopee and a great success in Afrique du Sud came irreversibly to an end. Most friends are gone; there are no more jobs, and all have left for greener pastures.

Z, the architect, poet, writer, and artist, listened to the seven-year call from his muse, who had passed on to the Big Void, as she used to call it. Z had seen good days with creative artwork, but the writing was on the proverbial wall.

My dear artist and poet who drifted from the profession of building with stone, clay, and concrete to the one that builds word-on-word stanzas and lyric poetry.

A process that'll need the same detailed care and meticulous attention, to summon the inner powers of creation and shape the verses to reach an aesthetical composition

LXXIII

To arrive back in one's country of birth
a shock at first to have left behind a life in art
at the doorsteps of his spiritual home
forego his collection of paintings and writings.

Oil paintings, acrylics, watercolours, drawings
all been taken for payment in lieu of cash
for the rental of a generous flat, en suite
for Mrs B and another part for ZG, the artist.

A compatriot muse recommended to call
the magistrate for social services in Vienna
who'll care for the needs of returning citizens,

who haven't been lucky enough to make it overseas,
who stranded while securing enough cash
to live on, but also failed as exhibiting artists.

LXXIV

Members of the Fine Arts School in Athens are
generous to foreign artists, well-qualified Europeans
however, Iannis, a senior member and a good guy to know
through my participation in a painter's seminar at Voula.

In close vicinity to the hospital, 'Dr Che,' as he's known
to the artist community, exhibits unknown artists
in his Art & Theatre Café. He's a surgeon but with
a great heart for struggling artists of exception.

Irene, Dr Che's secretary, is sweet and communicative
however, I could build an understanding immediately
she does the brochures for my exhibition in Voula

and later on also, in gallery Mi4d in Marousi, I met
Mrs A from a private gallery in Apo Glyfada helped me
to transport my paintings. There, I met Val, young and perky.

LXXV

Immediately, I took to her. She bought a painting
from me; I sold it at a discount. That's how our
friendship started and progressed to a deeper
understanding while she taught me Greek.

B, spouse, friend, partner in staying alive, battled with
her health, living at most times a stressful life, cutting off
suddenly all medication of psychosomatic pills,
prepared to fight through all symptoms of rejection.

However, Val, who wished to have children, I wouldn't
go along with, having been warned about this way
by my muse, of younger girls who live with their parents.

Indeed, how tricky it is to fall into the tender trap with
another obligation, when being married, does not count with
desperate girls who couldn't finish their academic studies.

LXXVI

Well, now, Val intended to seduce me but was inexperienced
and good for that. There is no way I would go the way of a
pal, a videographer of note, Anthony, the American, falling
for a Greek girl who had to marry with a child on the way.

He's part of a family, an average guy with two kids,
hooked on grass, living like the average Greek artist, he
introduce me to, smoking pot from a pipe, who came
from Sifnos Island and had lived in New York City.

Like most Greeks, America was their testing ground
learning new skills and where pain will spare
no mornings, no rush hour traffic jams, and no artists.

Anyone who wants to make a buck amid a flow of
metallic containers crowding all streets like locusts,
in humid air, red hot coal of summers, and winter's ice.

LXXVII

Meanwhile, I applied in Vienna for state support,
as a monthly, minimal rent would help to get on one's
two feet again, especially my partner, who never had
good luck with reaching the status of a regular income.

We took to the air and landed at the Vienna airport
we haven't seen for many years, with a rush of flocks of
strangers, an invasion of ants, this time from the Far East
in colours of many shades; we felt not entirely welcome.

But thanks to good angels, a woman explaining to me
how I should handle my unusual situation of return
of a compatriot Austrian to get settled again and live.

It was to live, look forward, and stay positive
find a small flat and start living as an artist and poet
while B began to seek out ways in fashion design.

pol drwg 11 – spouse & muse

LXXVIII

The poet who reads the poet's sonnets:
"Two joyous lovers have no end nor death
they are born and die many times while
living they have the eternity of nature

Inspired by the poet's sonnets, one of his
most favourite, he, zjg, poet and artist, is inspired
by Pablo Neruda's *100 Love Sonnets* he devoured
while recovering in a hospital bed.

At KOR LK, the hospital along the Danube, a fine,
skilled *operateur* removed his kidney stones that
developed for what reason? Nobody yet knows

until the lab results will fly in by e-Hermes and
the aged poet will then know how to conduct
his eating and drinking habits further.

LXXIX

The poet had flashes of memories and feedback to the
one most important question of his life: Why on earth
was his spouse not happy, although he had tried hard
to please her, both materially and sexually?

No, please stop Hypnos, don't give me impossible
dreams, but then, out of the dark blue night, in a flash
Aphrodite Knidos appeared, and the poet was gone
hook, line, and sinker. Telos. Well, what a Greek Fire.

No force on earth, no other woman could ever stop him
but his heart took his hand's soul, and both joined the
same couple of AK, the beautiful, the soulful, the passionate

"You know, if we carry on like this, we could have kids."
"Yes, yes," he sighed, and he came after she came, "pity we
are too old for that already," but why wasn't B that way?

LXXX

They both had the eternity of nature, a seed

passed into them by fate, but nobody had answers

only the bluebird of love cooing in the sycamore tree

the sweetness of fruit spicing up the song's desert.

But Ina appeared on cat paws and while singing in the

rain, pennies dropped from heaven, and the poet felt like

Joseph, being silvered, honoured by the pharaoh,

as another poet, the youngest Nobel Laureate put it.

with all these learned and successful poets, their muses

have to be honoured and adored, kissed and showered

with lots of love and appreciation, being counteractive

that they are friends, models, actresses, students, love

interests, mature women, partners for life's last rounds

of this earthly race on this blue, spinning planet.

LXXXI

At LK KOR, clinic extraordinaire, at room number five
there are three men of mature age besides the poet
who understands a few languages, German, Viennese,
Lower Austrian and some other local dialects

besides English, Hungarian, bits of Italian, and Greek.
But he is a man to listen rather than his opposite
neighbour, already a repeat patient and known to the
staff, while his curiosity nurtures a continuous monologue.

The old curious man, bed neighbour to a sportsman
in room no.5, the hottest room in the clinic's urology
department will follow up on all the new patients

knows god and the devil, offers his medical history
in his local dialect, next to him sporting Theo,
a marathon runner lives outside the wide open window.

LXXXII

There's a time at night when shadows emerge from the
smartphone's Internet pages and people become birds
or animals, plants are moving like magical illusions, faces look
into the room, black, pale, white, cinnabar, and soft yellow.

Mutations at the sound of a gong, then the night's spook
assembly turns into angelic humans in white dresses and
a blond woman in blue garb talks to me while I wash my
hands, feet, and face after recovering my carapace.

The mind knocked out the framed soul to Nomandsland,
soul's journey is a wondrous treat, as there's hope for
another round of a creative impulse for poetry.

Visions, music, panels of painting symbols of love and
death, a continual battle of words to be forged:
the hot, the cynical, the ridiculous, and the uplifting.

LXXXIII

Dreams of Africa, the clay cities, the not-united
states, the deep Southern Cape, the deserts,
the lion's might, the speed of gazelles, the Sufi
poets who inspire most-dreaded terrorists.

A vast continent where Europeans ventured
in good and evil, where life had been once
bearable for all until paradise was lost, not only
for Europeans, but also the local workforce

To talk about Africa, just as in any other continent,
one had to live there for some time, indeed!
And out of Africa, you came, and I desired you!

I loved and hated you. No, I loved an image, a mirage
and I couldn't preserve it, as it drove me to the edge
of expressing the imminent bushfire burn.

LXXXIV

Flung into the abyss of a nightmarish dream
I crossed the heart-shaped darkness of a continent
to find the love I have held so sweet in the palms
of my hands, but like a bluebird, I had to set it free.

How to survive a rubber band-pulling of a glowing
carapace that stretches by your hands, the towing
and throwing of a muse who attracted me
a powerful magnet that loved me to smithereens?

Now, in the wake of a Saturday morn' at 5:47 am
I felt the most incredible peace of my being to land
a comet that fell with the speed of light upon you.

Out of a nightmare of being pierced by needles of
searching for stones, I've carried for many years in my
body, a walking dead, saved by an eastern Gazelle.

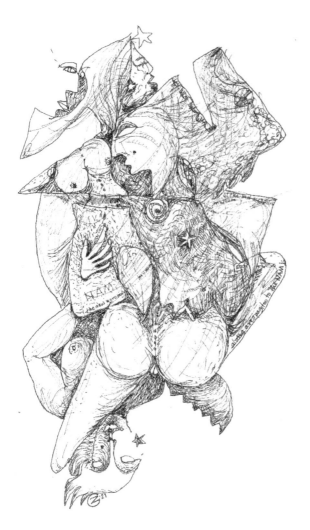

pol drwg.12 - the artist loves the NAM (New Acropolis Museum)

LXXXV

At 5:04 in the morn, Saturday 27th of the month
of July, you came to me, a muse, a lover, a spouse,
a mother, who would have thought it would be
this day of the seventh month of the year seven?

Indeed, my body woke up from dark moments
of death to be reborn; I took you into my arms.
I wanted you, the kissing, the chafing of skin to skin,
my lips aflame, my body heat in a flight with you.

The power of love at that point of seduction's heat
to give you my whole being in a gentle storm of
feelings will bring you to the boiling point in my wake.

Kisses on your body, from neck to bosom, roses, and
tulips, hibiscus opening for being a passionate flower
birds flick tongues for all-over devouring kisses.

LXXXVI

I tingled you like I tingled, imagining you, wishing
to seduce you, lapping the love of first intimacy,
besides, body stretching in a passion's rubber band
around the outskirts of Vienna's dark woods.

Around the mounds of the Kahlenberg, the vines,
the sweet juices, a spring of healing, nourishes me,
your slender legs in the air of a final embrace,
this time, the thunder of merging flesh and bones.

This time, the melting of souls, pine honey from
the native island that had prepared the unison,
a muse called Athina Knidos had started at Delphi,

at the short, intense union, highly erotic event
to continue for the poet of love who fell upon
the ground of Waterfield, second district, Vienne.

LXXXVII

For a long time, the stretched rubber band of a love
matured like the wine at the district cellars
it wound and wound an endless string of cotton
around the mummy of a poet, part of their dead society.

There were dreams of love, but not for a long time.
This early morn' it drove a wedge of sweet poison
into my heart of the cone where sweet honey would
stir, and well, in this reality, that's called LOVE.

Lost sparks of desire suddenly gathered like birds
that came back from the south to mate, rear their
offspring and stir feelings of love.

I've loved you for ages, for as long as I think back
from around the globe, from continent to
continent, from a first kiss, age is only a number.

LXXXVIII

Now I want you. Now I've found the Blarney Stone
of love that renders a man to have the gentle touches
I reshape your body with and with the love that
transfers lovers to another level.

A level of gentle flight surpassing gravity
the sweep of feelings, the cotton thread of a
spinning wind of hands, feet, torso and hips,
head and neck, belly and pussy, bums and back.

Wetted by the giant leaps of mind and soul
we have for years felt the libido's building up
couldn't think it would ever happen, but then?

It has happened in the mind this morn' of seven's,
figures that fell into our beings from the universe
and as oral love has filled our beings, we'll be alive.

LXXXIX

I look forward to the gardens of your Waterfield,
to the hibiscus mornings, days, and evenings,
whenever you sweep into the realm of my creative
aura and I will paint you with colours of love.

The voices of birds, animals, and humans have shaped
the background of a great canvas, love in a mature age
with mature lovers brought to sweet scents of
lovemaking to the cadenza of a blue bird's warble.

Sitting high in the silver-green foliage of a giant tree
on the porch of love's cosy cottage, created with the
mind of ever-driven Ina, an artist's refuge to stay alive

through creations that well up like volcanic desires
and will burst in ever-returning waves of fire and ice
like the creation of a new island in the Atlantic Sea.

XC

A symphony of love in the making, a long road
of trial and error, a consummate time for
surviving albeit traps of everyday life and past
errors of human nature, but found out about.

For knowing yourself is about to happen in a burst
of colours of a new spring and solidifying in the
landscape of autumn, like mature seasons for the
wine of hearts to solidify into a good wine.

It is that the poet has reached the breaking point
of the string that had been stretched to the edge
of holding him back, a wandering soul,

that has met another wandering soul he had
an intimate relationship in mind and soul
and at the edge of falling, falling in love.

XCI

A new life has just begun. Its promises are even
by the most cynical person, a light on the horizon's
darkening day, the cloud cover's blanket allows us to
celebrate despite a sad August afternoon.

The new life, given to the poet for an apparent reason,
as he has to write up his 100 and one sonnets, besides
his journal poetry, the trilogy of an artist's life
reflecting the sulphur-yellow, amber, and orange

of life's dramatic circles, the tow and throw of
love's fickle happenings, the high and mighty hours
of happiness, the deep, dark hours of desperation.

Though a new life can only start at the death of
an old life, one has to endure the pains of birth
perhaps these pains are more intense for a poet.

pol drwg.13 – palm tree

XCII

The old life is dead. It ceased in the Red Tower Room
during a whole night of writhing pain, I cried to the
muses to let me live until the early morn' to be able
to see a nearby doc' for some emergency medication.

Immediately after taking antibiotics for the painful
inflammation, a bladder colic? For the soul, muse Ina
ferried me to my Andrologist to initiate action and
medical care to get me back to good health.

Andrologist M-D's optical field disallowed a closer look
to see more detail of a place, a cavity, a nebula, where the
rock had hidden, causing so much aggravation and pain.

But at an ultrasonic inspection, Dr L saw some outlines of a
stone he thought could be in question; an angry muse must
have thrown at the poet in a sudden yellow rage.

XCIII

Immediately, alarm bells rang, and the poet had to undergo
a CT scan in the provincial city of Stockerau, where public
transport is laid back to say the least. What an odyssey to
detect the truth about a stone, goodness gracious.

At the end of a long night and day, Andrologist M-D
arranged for temporary help to keep away a rolling stone's
danger, avoid entry to hell, and stop at its forecourts
for the time being, and see the poet through purgatory.

"Yes, now as we know, there's one stone Blarney near death
we'll seek out the best way to remove it, but meanwhile
check with your stars if you'll have time to waste and draw!"

"Yes, I have; just please oil some levers and move my day
receiving a stent as near as possible to get it over with."
"Yes, I will do my best to see if I can get you a date soon."

XCIV

Thank you, dear Andrologist. Never mind, you didn't
notice the rock thrown by an angry muse, as my muses
are all women, jealousies happen all too frequently
and I was still in good luck with Dr L's discovery.

Well, now my old life will cease like the twilight's
slow darkening, and then the lights of hope will
be switched on, and the mind will work overtime
to have my 100+1 sonnets done in good time,

before I lie on a bed strapped like a crucifixion and
feel not a thing while the operateur searches thru
the urethra to fix me a stent for a future operation.

Not too many months to wait, but for three until a
hospital bed will become free, and the OP can start.
Have I walked all my life's pleasurable walks again?

XCV

Indeed, there's time for my OP, and I can't wait to
have this ordeal behind me. I write. At Waterfield, I
have a creative phase every time I'm here, every time
Ina will let me occupy her beloved cottage *a l'amour*.

The paradise's spittle, a wondrous place for an artist,
even his spouse acknowledges his change when he
returns. It's the place of soul bonding, a peaceful mind,
the bond of minds honed for love's upper layers.

Perhaps one day, the triad of love will be possible,
the poet wrote about something he experienced
at night, when he slept peacefully,

when his muse came to him, her mind power had
transformed her feelings; he felt physically so intense,
it happened to him also on a level of reality.

XCVI

He, the poet of love, Ana had called him, the poet of love
for Ina, who lives happily in his presence, but he hasn't yet
found the mood or the environment to love her
the way he had always dreamed about.

It will be, be patient; his inner voice hummed along
with the bluebird's singing on top of the fir tree in its
dusky crown, its needles like silver glitter at X-mas
in July. Everything is possible, my dear.

His inner voice is a brilliant keyboard of his muses
where a tune is played by whoever is in the mood
to leave a musical note for the poet's uplifting.

For the poet's happiness, as he loves his muses
and they take turns to love him, send him love notes
he'll transfer into a poem immediately.

XCVII

The operation is a success. "Never mind the blood
that flows from your inside," operateur Ghazel said.
Wonder Woman has saved the poet's life; he asks
her questions, and she answers them during a visit.

The poet listens, reads up on her personality, and
then learns that there are love poems called Ghazels.
How interesting, a woman called 'Love Poems' saved
the life of a Poet of Love! Indeed!

This means that there's a lot of hope, and now
the poet is already up on the second day, taking
his pen and writing another few sonnets of love.

Love is all I need. Love is all Ina will need, he muses.
This is the new life. This is all that Ana had already
prophesized to him when their love ended tragically.

XCVIII

Z, Zen, Zeni, Zsolt, poet and artist, is fulfilled writing
his poems, sonnets, prose poems, journal poems,
ballads, Ghazels, short stories, novels, memoirs, and
Belle Letters has his road ahead mapped out.

I, Ina, Inanna, Iris, the poet's muse and sponsor,
the secret love interest of the poet, yet Ina had
not placed more interest in it, as she believes both
have lived their lives already; their hubbies still alive.

Perhaps at her limits in psychic and emotional terms,
the poet has a gut feeling, quite poignant indeed.
All Ina lacks is a triad of love; the man is Z, the poet.

Z with his ability to make her a woman again. Never
mind age; it's a number. There are erotic plays that'll
catapult lovers at any age into the stratosphere of love.

XCIX

The dusk settled like the eyes that closed
and slowly blanked out daylight. There's love
at this time on the white leather skin of
animals, smooth and seductive to lie upon.

The room turns at an angle, and the mind
draws a few lines into a portrait of a loved one
from this world or the past. It is beautiful
and animates the surface of the poet's skin.

He'll embrace legs and thighs and samples
with his lips, toes, muscles, and supple skin,
and works his way up his muse's tender thigh

to the point of heat and sea salt and oysters
there's sun and the lapping of the sea, like licks
of love that spices up a love long dormant.

C

These happenings are as accurate as day and night
in the new life of the poet, the trail of happiness
is in every fling at all times, the touches, the gazing
into each other's eyes when sharing a meal.

The driving together along city roads, the loose
conversation of nearness, the sweet nothings
that float between them, Ina's pursed lips, the
glances in her eyes and the soft tone of her voice.

The way she wears a dress, Emilia Flöge style
that shows her slender legs crossing them for
the poet observes, works his way up; she knows

teasing and touching, not yet sweet kissing
but close enough to happen soon, lips-to-lips
skin to skin, tongue-touches to tongue-touches.

pol drwg.14 – dusk settled seamlessly as the eyes closed

CI

It's a beautiful new life, it is. The skin warms with her
touches. The feet feel like walking on coals, and the whole
body is on fire. It trembles like silver poplar leaves
when the dry, high grass around it has caught fire.

There's no quick ending of a climax, awaiting the times
when they could live together, alone; it's a long road
to Tipperary of Tantric love's union for both of them
having mentally committed to each other many years back.

The poet remains stealthy, having practiced self-love
to know himself intimately, so he'll bide his time to get
to know Ina that way, muscles, heart, and personality.

Whatever it takes, he'll always be there for her, and
she knows it, being at his side, officially and unofficially.
There are good days in free spirits and the wine of love.

*

Index

Page   Content

About the author

Born in eastern Austria, close to the Hungarian border, he witnessed as a young man the horrors of a nation's brutal suppression, erupting in the Hungarian Revolution of 1956. He finished his education in art and architecture in Vienna, married, and sailed for the Cape of Africa, an adventure that followed his childhood dreams. He had drawn African animals for his art classes, but the time had come to see them in their natural habitat.

Meeting a varied facet of people and cultures, working as a draughtsman in an engineering office, and as an architect for a cultural centre, he made good use of his language skills travelling throughout Southern Africa.

During a trip to Lesotho, a native artist showed him rock paintings with their stark palimpsest outlines and typified movements of animals and humans. These paintings made a lasting impression on him and influenced his artistic work.

His vast collection of drawings and slides had been lost during a change of domiciles, but further studies of the San people would reawaken his dormant artistic longing for the expression of his art, filling sketchbooks with drawings and notepads with poetry and prose.

While revisiting the capitals of Europe, he sensed that the bond of art, being borderless and free, would reach across continents into the world.

During a visit to Greece, he was accepted into a circle of artists and poets who encouraged him to continue his art. A poetess introduced him to the works of famous Greek poets.

In South Africa, he joined the writing and poetry workshops of Writers Write. It was to open the floodgates to his creativity. He decided to travel through Greece and visit its sites of antiquity, read up on Classical mythology, and enjoy first-class translations of Greek poetry and prose.

He settled in 2023/14 in Klosterneuburg-Weidling. Poet Nikolaus Lenau is buried here. Franz Kafka had visited here. Their writings will always be an inspiration.

Other books by the author:

(Available at BoD-Books on Demand /bookshop, Norderstedt, and all major bookshops, as E-book or in print)

In English:

Acropolis – Book I, Fervour

Athens Elegies – A Poet's Lament

Cantos Libidos – Love's Pure Emotion

Clouds I – Dancing Eros

Clouds II – Wing Child Eros

Diary of an Aged April – a month in the life of a poet on the
                Southern hemisphere

Educating Pizzy – The Artist Evolves

Elegy of an Unusual Peak, Book I – Real and Virtual Loves

Elegy of an Unusual Peak, Book II – Days in Love

Fighting Stance – Triangulation in Love

King of Ice – A Poetic Legend

LOVE & ART I – Songs of Passion, First Volume

LOVE & ART II – Songs of Passion, Second Volume

MUSES – The artist between heaven and hell

MUSES II – The artist in the Muse's garden

MUSES III – Waking in Love

MUSES IV – Magic Unisons

Poetry in times of lockdowns and isolation, Book I –
                Missing the City's Hub

Poetry in times of lockdowns and isolation, Book II –
                The City Deserted

POETRY OF THE INNERMOST Book I – Colour Scales of Love

POETRY OF THE INNERMOST Book II – In Praise of Mature
                Women

Red Tower Room – A Poet's Refuge